Sweet and Bitter Twisted

About the Author

Semba Jallow-Rutherford is a Sociology graduate who lectures in equal opportunities within the field of further education. His life experiences within both his professional and personal domain have brought greater depth to his work and his singular insights into the foibles and idiosyncrasies of his fellow travellers through the miasma of life, have become more evident in this his second volume of poetry.

Semba's previous anthology - Chapters In Life, published in 1997 has led to a much wider audience being privy to his unique and enlightening style through radio, media and popular public interest. He is now heard and read locally, nationally and internationally and is a distinguished life member of the International Society of Poets.

SWEET AND BITTER TWISTED

BY
SEMBA JALLOW-RUTHERFORD

Date of Publication
1998

© Semba Jallow-Rutherford
All rights reserved including
the rights of reproduction

Published by:
JARU Publications
PO Box 6915
Birmingham
B32 2LF

Printed by:
MAS Print & Design Ltd
Unit B3 Windmill Works
Peartree Lane
Dudley
West Midlands
DY2 0UY

ISBN 0 9530 6725 4

Acknowledgment

Special praises go to the Energy Source from whence I get my inspiration and the ability to pen my thoughts and observations.

A very special thank you goes to Junior *Jallow*-Grant for coming up trumps with a beautiful cover design and for being there for me through my highs and lows. To Jane Palmer for her support and suggestions throughout and for having the nerve to put a pile of poems into some kind of arrangement for the book. To Gloria Spence for her wonderful support and friendship, albeit from afar. To Andy and Diane for sorting me out a 'special' writing desk. To James Smith for his enduring encouragement throughout. To Sanua Linton for friendship and keeping me going when I had my doubts. And last but by no means least, to everyone who gave me the conviction to continue writing and directly or indirectly helped me to compile this anthology.

Dedicated to my father

Elijah Rutherford

Who was not lucky enough to see
neither my name nor his in print.

Daddy may the source be with you
Wherever you are

CONTENTS

	Page No
Foreword [Invisible]	1
Just Ice	5
Confused States	7
Man to Man	8
Seeking Soulful Moments	9
Cynicism	10
Who Cares For Him	12
Black Man's Pride	14
Laws of the Land	15
Battles Of Our Fathers Land	17
For Labi	18
Proud To Be Black	19
Wake Up Black Men	21
Laughing and Crying	25
Energy and Beauty	27
Humanity	28
Spirituality	30
Waiting [for your letter]	31
Misery	32
Pethidine [1]	33
Pethidine [2]	34
Voices of Colour	35
Black Man/Beggar Man	37
Stand Up	38
Take Heed	40
The Blues In Jazz	41
He Said	43
In A Dream Maybe	44
Recognition	45
Rebel	46
Sweet And Bitter Twisted	51
Pained Tears of A Woman	53
Hold Me	54
Power Of The Flower	56
Wings Of Love	57
Who Are You	58

Loving U Is Easy	60
Alone And Isolated	61
Kwi	62
For You	63
Empty Space	64
Give A Little Piece Of You[FOR POPS]	66
Butterfly	69
You All	70
Realization	72
Human Sponge	74
The Birthday Poem	75
Let Me Be	76
Thanks	77
Bleats Of Sheep	78
Dizzy On Thin Air	79
Dancing In The Breeze	80
The Haunting	81
Tell Me Why	82
Brawn Not Brain	85
A Way To Change	86
Fold Me Away	87
Sound And Vision	89
Different Worlds	91
Sunshine Smile	95
Christmas Cheers	96
Searching For Self	97
Rain In Tunisia	98
Prosperity	99
Words	100
Fun Times Alone	101
Atlanta Morn	102
The Journey	103
She Spoke My Name	104
Life Is A Moving Thing	109
Poem For Alan [Gin And Tears]	110
Ode For Alan	111
Thoughts For Rose	113
Don't Do It	114

FOREWORD

INVISIBLE

They stare at me
But they do not see me
They talk about me
As if I am not there
They are polite in my presence
But they ignore me
They see my body
But they don't see me
They brush pass me
But they don't touch me
They know I am here
They feel my presence
But they deny me
My existence

They are not blind
But they can't see me
They are not deaf
But they can't hear me
They have the sense of touch
But they cannot feel me
They do not want me
So they deny my being here
They don't want me
Yet they need me
As long as I am made
To stay
INVISIBLE

oh what bitterness
is left after the sweetness
of your tenderness

JUST ICE
(A TRIBUTE TO STEVEN LAWRENCE)

You call me a militant for fighting
For my rights to exist in your racist system
You call me a militant because what you call justice
I call Just Ice, cold and ephemeral
You in your Just Ice system try to reduce
Me in the multiple to a life of worthlessness

I have news for you Mr. Just Ice maintainer
I have me a voice
In fact we have voices in the many
Forced to scream for justice not Just Ice
Fighting for our human rights
To be valued as a people
For you to recognise that the taking of a
Black man's life is as important as that of a
White man's life
You Mr. Just Ice man need a Little Heat
For to warm your cool, cold heart
In the hope you might melt into a little
humanity
we don't want speacial treatment of your sympathies
Just what is good and well in your rather
unjust system
I have to shout out load and let the people
know
Of what is going on in your repressive system

You damned me for daring to speak of the killing
Of a young black man
Because my voice is full of rage and acrid bitterness
Which if not spit out is likely to choke me
And in doing so it will set you free
Mr Just Ice man, I will not be your punching bag
I will stand up straight and strong
I will scream and shout or rant or rave
Or fight you tooth and nail to get what it is I want
You better start to re-plan your strategies
For I will not stop fighting you

Until you make the killing of my black mother's son
As important as the killing of your own white son

Don't be afraid of my shouting voice
Listen carefully to what it is I want, you hear
Concentrate and you might hear that what I want is
Justice
Not Just Ice
From one who supposedly refers to himself
As the son of Jesus Christ

CONFUSED STATES

If I am
Me
Myself

How can I
Be a part
Of
You
Us
Is
You
And
Me
Myself and I

After all
I am me
Not a part of you
And you are you
Not a part of me

Why do we struggle to be
A part of what we physically cannot be
Why can't we accept
That
You are you
And
I am me
Hence
Allow
Us to be
Who we rightfully are and
sound be

MAN TO MAN

Man yu a chat mi to deat'
an' wi naa get no weh
Yu a burs' mi ears
an' a dry mi tears
an' all dem kin' a t'ings

man...
yu a burs' mi ears
an' a tek mi time.
Fi all mi know...
yu good fi a tell me lies

man...
mi need some sleep
jus' fi res'mi eyes
an' mi need some sleep
to kin' a fin' mi space
an' fin' miself

far fram the deepest thicket
of the sharpest thorns
where I can lie
'till morn
at the break of dawn

where the toads will spawn
in the open pond

man .yu fi t'ink sometimes
an' mek an action plan
work on it...
an' no waste your time.

Don't waste your time
and then you won't waste mine

Man ...
yu a chat mi to deat'
an' yu waste mi time.

SEEKING SOULFUL MOMENTS

You don't have to travel far
Not to the station let alone the star
Soulful moments can be obtained
From that place in that moment right where you are
Soulful moments were there at the time of your creation
They have been there for many generation
Soul can be found in the garden or in the park
In the light as well as in the dark
Soul is present in the singing of the birds
So too are they in the written or in the spoken words
Soulfulness is found in the animals be they caged or wild
As in the seasons whether it be harsh or mild
Soul is to be found in the sun that shines
It can also be found in this little heart of mine
Soul can be found among your friends and companions
Seek, search for yourself, this is only my opinion
For I believe that soul is always very near
Whether it be here or there - it is everywhere

CYNICISM

New year new start
old way old days
new shoes new clothes
old smiles old wears.

Happy New Year
drinks talk
all grins
no frills
ting, ting,
the telephone rings
Happy New Year

What will it bring
New things
Chatter, chatter
tongues wagging
lips smacking
bottles and glass gets clattering

Silence, then
Will all acquaintance
be forgot and never ....
then comes screaming
and shouting
of 'happy new year'
bow, bow,
fire-works sparking
and lit the sky
with a certain knowing.

Then I looked and saw
the same old stars
in the old cloud, shining.

People walking, hugging and kissing
uttering the words

What's changed..
 Anything
 then I wonder
 if this year,
the circle, will be unbroken.

WHO CARES FOR HIM

Who cares about Semba Jallow
who really gives a damn
whether he lives or if he dies
split in many pieces
he shares himself among those
who demand a piece of him
who cares about Semba Jallow
who gives a shit about him

You each take a part of him
whenever you demand
you take from him
his voice
advice
his heart
his words
even his very thoughts
who gives a damn about Semba Jallow
who gives a shit about him.

He shares his all
with each of you
and tells you all take heed
you must remember thou dear fellows
that even he has needs.
Who gives a damn about Semba Jallow
do you really care.

You take his time
advantage of his kindness
and his ever willingness
to share his all with you
but do you really care about him
do you really care
Who gives a damn about Semba Jallow
Do you care about him.

Many a times his house is full
someone, somewhere, wanting part of him

no one thinking ever
he might want, or even need a part of them
so, who gives a damn about Semba Jallow
and, do you really care.

He gives, and gives and gives again
and all you do is take
believing that he can not see
that most of you are fake
so, do you give a damn for Semba Jallow
tell me, do you care for him.

In darkened space, he sits alone,
dejected,
unloved
and unwanted
once all your needs are met
so do you give a damn about Semba Jallow
Do you really care for him.

Tell me truly do
Do you know about his agonising
and his tortured years
do you ever see his sullen eyes
or his sallow look
ever think of returning
some of what you take from him
so how can you care about Semba Jallow
how can you care for him.

BLACK MAN'S PRIDE

Black man get up from the gutter
Black man don't hang your head in shame
Black man hold your head up high
Black man carry yourself with pride

Black man do you really want to be free
Black man look to yourself B 4 U look to me
Black man are you doing all you can
To free yourself from the bottom of the pile
Black man

Black man there is no need to hide your face
Black man stand up and be proud of your race
Black man get yourself together and make an action plan
Black man pull yourself out of the gutter man

Black man stand strong for your black woman
Black man remember your black children
Black man work hard both for you and them
Black man be a role model for all our children
Black man.

LAWS OF THE LAND

Look after me and I'll treat you right
Say land to man and man to land
Feed and nurture me and I'll do the same for you

Land to man

Plough me, weed me, water me and feed me
And I'll grow you
Food for energy
Trees for shelter
Grazing for your domesticated beasts

I will provide a place for creatures rare and wild
I will feed and house them proudly in my little haven
I want you to put back in me that which you take away
So I can continue to keep you nourished
And house you comfortably

Man to land

Let us live harmoniously
In your scape of beauty
Shelter me from harm
And care for me protectively
In this my selected spot of beauty
You so green and lush

So hot
So strong
So sure
So steady

Teach me how to be at peace with you
Oh, oh great land of beauty
So loved and circled by the sea
You so full of hills and plains
Covered by star lit sky at night
I'll give you that which you desire

So we can live together
In harmony
Peaceably

Dependent on each other totally

BATTLES OF OUR FATHERS' LAND

And still we fight
    The battles of yesteryear
        We fight a battle
            Commenced before our birth
                We fight
a battle
            Which
will continue
        After we've
ceased to be
        We fight
the battle
        On unleveled
battleground
        We fight the
battle
    That we have to win
      We fight the battle
        That we can not lose
           We fight the battle
              O'er the MOTHER
LAND
                We fight the
battle
      For our
FATHERS' LAND
              We fight the
battle
        Across the diaspora
        We fight the battle
      We have to fight

FOR LABI

What a man
What a night
What a mystery
On this night
You revealed to me

I did not know
Labi
About your chequered
History
Is it history
Or is it really simply
Your story

From early on
You had to fight
And fought you did
For many
The battles you have won

With your words
Labi
You speak for ME
And ME and ME
Though you may feel
You wrote for YOU
And only YOU

From the audience
I pat your back
From my base
I check your lyrics
With my friends
I sing your praise
And tell them
That you are free
For freedom lies with you
LABI
LABI SAFFRE

PROUD TO BE BLACK

Born a black babe
To a black woman
In a black homeland

I talk black talk, in my black tongue
To a black race on a black island

Now a black man living in a white land
I talk black talk to the white race
And the black ones

Proud to be BLACK
That is why I spend my time
Fighting back
'Cause we are proud to be BLACK

Mi dance black dance
Mi mek black noise
Mi talk black talk
Mi fite de racis' back
To show I'm proud to be BLACK

Mi form black groups
Mi fite fi mi rites
Mi naa stan back
Tek no racis attack
Mi a move up front
An a fite dem back
Fite de buggers back
Why tek dem racis attack
Dem nu de master race
But share disgrace
To de human race
Fite dem back an' stay
Proud to be BLACK

All you out there
Don't know who you are
Join black groups and fight race war

Don't let yourselves be governed by
Divide and rule
Join black groups and find yourselves
Join black groups and know who you are
Join black groups
And show you are
Proud to be BLACK

Marcus Garvey was
Proud to be BLACK
Martin Luther King was
Proud to be BLACK
Malcolm X was
Proud to be BLACK
Bob Marley was
Proud to be BLACK
Louis Farakhan is
Proud to be BLACK
You are proud to be BLACK
I am proud to be BLACK

So don't stand back
An' tek no racis attack
Fite dem back
An' stay proud to be BLACK

WAKE UP BLACK MEN

See her standing there
See the mask she wears
Passed on to her by her mothers
Like their mothers before them did

Now just you watch her smile
Watch her as she stares
See those tensions that she make
The indentations in the mask
Watch those lines of pain
That show her experiences

She carries the burdens of her ancestors
And bears the pain of our mothers
Watch her as she smiles
And the pain within her lies

See how well she wears her mask
Can you recognise her face
Or is she a faceless person
The ones we see everyday
Wearing the mask she wears so well

Did you see her yesterday
When she unveiled her well worn mask
Did you see the sternness
On her face
She so representative of her race
Carries the pains of our nation

In her face I see the barriers
Sense her defiance
And an emergence of a new found confidence

She is the black woman
Tired of her fighting
Sick of wearing the mask
Dares to show her strength

Willing to take on her assailants
Psyched and ready for war
On the white race
On the black man

The woman is tired
Of living different lives
Of hiding behind her mask
She is angry with her black man
For running away from her
Leaving her to fight alone
And rear their hungry children
And leaving her in the cold with them

Can you not feel her strength
And her determination
No longer hiding
She freely unveils her mask
Can't you sense her courage
As she fights alone
Ignored by the white woman
Oppressed by the white race
And her own black man

Look out black men
you'll not escape her wrath
Watch out white race
You'll be devoured single handed
Take heed black men
And help your black women

births bring happiness
deaths leave many people hurt
healing comes through pain

LAUGHING AND CRYING

Laughing, laughing, laughing,
Life sweet sah
Laughing, laughing, laughing,
What a sweet thing life really is
Yesterday, I heard you say
Life is good and well
When all is well with love

Laughing, laughing, laughing,
Isn't life really sweet
When we have food enough to eat
When the sun bears down on us
It's heat
When we have full use of our
Hands and feet

Life is really sweet
When all in life is going well

It's unlike me to spoil your fun
When life for you is having a good run
But my laughter turned to tears
This morning
When I heard of another killing
By a group of K K K young animals
Who have no place among the human race

They killed my brother, my father, my friend
And yes, some of us are crying
Whilst I know that some of you are laughing
Others are laughing and crying at the same time
Not for or at the gruesome killing
Of the rather young James Byrd
No that would just be too absurd

Some of us are laughing and crying
Because of the sweet and bitter things
That happen to them in this life

Yes life can be sweet
But it can be bitter too

Right now, I don't feel like laughing
But if you do, it's completely up to you

ENERGY AND BEAUTY

Energy comes from all around me
Those who love as well as hate me
From the grain of wheat which sustains me
The water from the tap or in the sea
Rays of sun which shine and warm me
The rain that falls and quench the thirsty soil

Beauty comes from inside of me
It shows itself in all I do
Beauty my friend also comes from you
It's in the birds flying high and free
It's in the shrubs as well as in the trees
It's in your homes and not your houses
In the leaves as well as in the roses

Energy and beauty is in you and me

HUMANITY

Come on people
Stop the warring
All we're asking
is the ending of
Useless killing

Come on brothers
join our sisters
In their campaigns
Against destruction
Of our environ

Come on fathers
Join our mothers
Against the slaughter
Of our children

Come on soldiers
Quit the slaying
Of innocent people
Stop the wasting
Of beautiful lives.

If I was a soldier
I would down my weapon
Fingers off the trigger
Make myself a winner

Come on soldiers
Down your weapons
With love
And not with hate

Why don't we together
Stop the warring
Stop the hating
End the fighting
And cease the killing

Why don't we together
Let the blood flow
And give peace a chance
In this warring land
Where we can try
To live in perfect harmony

What we are saying
Is stop the warring
For we don't want the killing
Of our little ones

Come on world leaders
Meet with your opponents
Try alternatives to the marring
Of the children's' future.

SPIRITUALITY

Plant your feet upon the ground
Dig them deep so they may take
Spurt long roots and grow up strong
Dig your toes like roots and make them spread
Hold your-self up straight and strong
Like the well rooted tree you ought to be

With your feet planted in the earth
And your head near to the sky
Raise your hands with fingers spread
Waver them
Like branches on the human tree
Shake your head and let your hair fall
Like leaves beating as they waver in the trees

Lift your-self and let your head fall
Pillowing itself on your supportive shoulders
As you look skyward to the heavens which lie above
Open up your heart
And let your soul smile with your God
Who lets the sun shines down on your face

Stand firm upon the ground
Transfixed to mother earth
Smile and show your grace
In the fullness of its glory therewith

Through your breathing
Let your secrets known
in coded breaths as it passes in the wind
Send your calming thoughts
In the rushing of the leaves
As they waver in the trees

WAITING
[FOR YOUR LETTER]

I've been waiting a long, long time
for that letter you promised me
everyday the postman called
I dashed for the letter box
shook my head and think of my favourite song

'No letter today'

Maybe tomorrow then
but - will tomorrow ever come
tomorrow is anoder day,
de day afta dis ya one.

After this morning
I made a move to get a pen
held it in my hand
an' den staat to t'ink 'bout it
wha mi a go sey
T'ink I betta write
a letta to you instead.

Now de pen in a mi 'an
paper on the desk
and nottin in a mi 'ead

So think I better sit and wait
for de pos' man
to drop yours instead

MISERY

Something inside makes him a man possessed
He says it's a pain you cannot pluck
He is so weak, he has no strength to fight
It's like a cancer you can not cut
He says, it is a pain that wants to be crushed
It's like a prison that's holding him in
At times, he wants to dismantle himself
Sometimes he even screams out and shout
He talks of pain like electrical spark
Which thumps and kicks like a thunder from hell
Why him he asks
But there is nought anyone can tell

PETHIDINE [1]

I am a noise
a sound
an echo
inside my head

The globe
a universe
engulfed my being

my thoughts
echoes
rebounds
...............in sounds.

I float like cloud
supported by air
I breathe silently
yet loud,
softly,
yet I scream.

On a bed of
cloud
I lie,
and like a bird,
oh, in my head,
I fly
I fly.

PETHIDINE [2]

One little pill

white and plain

that's all it takes

to ease my pain

That little pill

small though it is

has the strength

of a horse

and the sting

of a bee.

It picks me up

and make me float

then gently let me down

to a crash

and a bang

to my life of pain

and then I sink

VOICES OF COLOUR

Raise your voices and be heard
you invisible ones
Raise your voices in your praises
to the holy one
Lift yourselves to higher ground
and make your voices heard

Put your colours
yourselves and everything
Into voices which will be heard
by those too blind to see
Though they have in them
the gift of vision

Make sounds of colours
in unison
Paint rainbows with all that you have
Let yourself be seen
by those who wish to dismiss
Your very being

Reach out and touch
with your finger tips
Sing praises and run them off
with your gifted lips
Sing praises and
let yourselves be praised

Touch the hearts of those
so full of hatred
Touch their ears
with your gifted hands
Sing out loud sing out clear
sing my loves so that all can hear

Touch them let them feel
your hands upon their prickly skin
Breathe on them
so they may feel your breath
Move objects so they will know
that you are here

Sing colours
so they will begin to visualise

BLACK MAN/BEGGAR MAN

Hey, what do you think you're doing
'bout you're begging
stop the scrounging
and instill a sense of pride

Hold your head up high
and look fully right in their eyes
not to the earth with your eyes cast down
look at them with your ever smiling eyes
not through them now you hear

Black man stop the begging
and the scrounging
learn new skills and use them wistfully
educate yourself so you can teach me
how to survive

Black man teach you
so you can teach our children

STAND UP

How much longer will you lie on the ground
and let yourself be beaten
How much longer will you resign yourself
to live with lies
How much longer will you let yourself
be trampled on
How much longer will you let yourself be crushed

How much longer
How much longer

I say stand up now and face things like a man
Stand up now and show the strength of woman
Show them children that you are the adults for tomorrow

How much longer will you show your endless patience
How much longer can you turn the other cheek
How much longer will you let yourself be humiliated
How much longer can you sit alone and cry

How much longer
How much longer

I say stand up and show unitedness
I say stand up if you are sick of being crushed
I say stand up in strength and togetherness

How longer will you let yourself be oppressed
How much longer will you go on feeling helpless
How much longer will you let your views be brushed aside
How much longer will live and suffer in silence

How much longer
How much longer

I say stand up and face your enemies
I say stand up and don't resign yourself to failure
I say stand up and let your legs support you

How much longer can you be all forgiving
How much longer will you let yourself be stood on
How much longer will stay weak and passive
How much longer will you hide your scars and bruises

How much longer
How much longer

I say stand up and face your oppressors
I say stand up and expose them for their weakness
I say stand up and end their evilness

How much will you be a doormat
How much will you be a punching bag
How much will you suffer in silence
How much longer will you protect that bastard

How much longer
How much longer

I say stand up and show them that you mean business
I say stand up and show you're not afraid of them
I say stand up and let yourself be counted

I say stand up
I say stand up

TAKE HEED

Oppressor man take heed
And stop your brutalising
Oppressor man take heed
And try control your greed

For time a go come
When we naa tek no more
Time a go come
When we will whip your ass for sure
Time a go come
When we have to end your cruelty and strife

World controllers
Don't abuse your powers
World controllers
Remember to feed your people

For time a go come
When you fall from grace
Time a go come
When you'll need some help
Time a go come
When you need support

World leaders lead right
And don't try to rule by terror
World leaders try and listen
To those who place you
On your ivory towers

For time a go come
When you can't lead no more
Time a go come
When you're going to be judged
Time 'ave fi come
When you'll be over-thrown
Time a go come
When you must take account
For your action.

THE BLUES IN JAZZ

Sing for me oh Lady Day
Sing for me whether you will or may
Sing for us because
You are the blues
In jazz
Because
You are the blues
Of jazz

                June and me we talked
                  Of Carmen McRae
                      And you
                    Billie Holiday
                      Because
                We wanted to find
              Who was the blues
                      In jazz
              Who was the blues
                    of jazz

                                We knew it could not be
                                        Nina Simone
                                  For she is the jazz
                                            In jazz
                              She is undoubtedly
                                      The voice
                                          Of jazz

Sing for us oh
Carmen McRae
Sing for us
Whether you will or may
Because
You could be
The blues
Of jazz
You're the blues
Of jazz

What about you Sarah Vaughn
Could you be the jazz in blues
Why don't you give a note or two
As we try to find the
Jazz of blues

Ella you're renown
As the jazz of jazz
Never mistaken for the
Blues of jazz
For when you scat
That's perceived as the
Real razzmatazz
The jazz of jazz

HE SAID

He said
I cannot love
For I
Was not fed on love and kisses
I cannot love
For my soul
Is so very cold
I cannot love
For no one took the time
To teach me how
So he said
He'll teach me love
He'll hold me in ready arms
Outstretched in readiness
For long haul flight
He'll take my heart
And warm it in his hands
He said
He'll take my tear ducts
Touch them gently
And teach me how to cry
If he can
I think
That he should try

IN A DREAM MAYBE

DADDY
Why don't you come to me
no more
You don't sit on my shoulders
Like you used to do before
You don't come
You don't call
Messages to me
You no longer send

Is it because
My visits to your resting place
are few
I don't bring flowers
Like I used to do
I don't clear the weeds and grass
Like I ought to do

DADDY
I long to see
your smiling face
and hear the laughter
in your sweet soft voice
I see you sometimes
among the living
Who knoweth not
I thing of you

Do you
Or do you not know
You're with me more dead
Than when you were living

Reach me some time
In a dream may be
Let me remember how sweet
Your presence can be
Reach out your hands
And call to me
For soon it will be
Another anniversary

RECOGNITION

I'm not my body
My body is not me
I've let my body
Floating by the sea

I am a wandering spirit
That's who I am
I am a feeling being
That's trapped within

I am made of cells
And genes and bones
Padded with flesh
With lots of blood
Flowing through my veins

My body is here
And I am there
I float free
And wander far
I'm here and there
I get everywhere

I float along
Singing a brand new song
I glide through space
A member of
The universe

A member of
The human race
A member of
The spirit world
A member of
The human kind.

REBEL

Rebel, rebel
Rebel, rebel, rebel
They call me a rebel
But I am not that gullible
Rebel, rebel
Rebel, rebel, rebel

I'll fight my rights
But I'm no rebel really
I'll challenge
The oppressors
But does that make me a rebel

Rebel, rebel
Rebel, rebel, rebel
That is because I fight back
They call me rebel
Why that is I cannot tell
Rebel, rebel
They call me rebel

I haven't the fame of Mohammed Ali
Nor the courage of Marcus Garvey
I cannot sing like Bob Marley
Yet they call me a rebel
Yes rebel

I speak my mind and I am a rebel
I strike them back and they call me rebel
I organise me and they call me rebel
What is it that makes me a rebel

You ride my back and I rebel
You call me names and I rebel
You pressurise me and I am rebel
Rebel, rebel
Rebel, rebel, rebel

You patronise me I challenge that
I show you strength you bruise my ego
I heal myself and still you call me a rebel
A REBEL
ME A REBEL, REBEL, REBEL

campari bitter
taste of honey much better
boozers lives twisted

SWEET AND BITTER TWISTED

Should loving you be wrong
Because of who you are and who I am
Should loving you be wrong
Because of where you and I come from
Should loving you be wrong
Because of our ebony and ivory skins
Should loving you be wrong
When my heart says right
And my head tells me that I am wrong

If I should let myself love you
Like my heart says I ought to do
Will you understand the me
When I am in agony deep
Caused by the many isms
In your parochial system
Could you truly love me
When I am hurt and angry
Can you soothe my pains and scars
When you are among the ones
At whom my anger is vented

Can you through love
Allow yourself to feel my injured mind
Could you try to see the world
From my perspective
Should loving you be wrong
When we are brothers under skin
Should loving you be wrong
When we each other emotionally feed
Should loving you be wrong
When I willingly give myself to you
Can loving you be right
When I am sweet and bitter twisted

If loving you is wrong
Can you say
What to do about my inner feelings
If loving you is wrong

Can something be done to make it right
Can I truly love you and your ivory skin
Before I learn to love me and my ebony one
Can I love my neighbour
Before I learn to love me and my ancestries
Can you love me truly, like you love yourself
Tell me this if you will
Can I love you
Before learning to love me first
If I can
Can you please, please tell me how

PAINED TEARS OF A WOMAN

Weep no more please
Don't weep no more
The hurt for which you cry your tears
May be caused externally
But the cure for your injuries
Lies inside of you

Weep no more I ask you please
Stop to think of how you are hurting you
And s\he who still within you reside
Your cure my friend is well within your grasp

Weep no more
In your pregnant state
Your baby needs you to be strong
Now it's arrival time to join you
Will now not be long

Weep no more
I plead with you
And try to touch your hurt
Organise your mind
Make yourself a mental list and get it checked

Weep no more
Your 'J' is still with you
Weep no more
For he is weeping too.

HOLD ME

You told me to
Hold you
Touch you
Feel you
Love you
Cuddle you

You told me to tell you
How much I love you
Now I want you to
Hold me
Touch me
Feel me
Love me
Cuddle me

And you're not here
You are over there
Being cuddled by somebody else

Now you tell him
To hold you
Feel you
Touch you
Cuddle you
Love you
And embrace you
Now I want you to
Touch me
Kiss me
Caress me
Fondle me
And love me
And you are not here
You're over there
Doing these to someone else
You told me
You'ld be there for me
'till the end of time

Now I'm here alone
Wanting you
To hold me
Kiss me
Whisper
Sweet nothing to me
And you're out of here
Over there
Doing just what
You want to do

POWER OF THE FLOWER

For you my love
Steps are taken to my garden
In the flower bed
I searched amongst the roses
There I saw the ones
That made me think of you
For on their stems
I saw a million you
In colours of the rainbow
And on their stems
Their lingered scents
Reminds me of that which you leave behind
When you leave me in an empty room
These flowers in my hand I hold for you
Petals perfectly formed
I'll dry and press
To protect their perfectness
And when I think of you
I'll hold them up to my
Nose and my breast
In the hope my love
They will fill my emptiness.

WINGS OF LOVE

Take me to that place where nobody cries
Where nobody worries
To all smiling faces
Where all races mingle
I say take me there
On your wings of love
In protective arms
Please, please take me there

Love, oh love
Let me follow you
To the place where
I'll be glad and happy
And live in harmony
With everyone around me
Please, please take me
To that rainbow land
Where all is great and grand

Far, far from ghetto land
Where aching tired feet
I can lay to rest
And sweet peace I shall greet
Oh come and take me there
Where I can be with you
Together endlessly

Come and take me there
To that place where
Nothing ever dies
Where people live in peace
With nature easily
Come and take me there
On your feathered wings of love

Or wings of mine
So I may fly

To that land
Where all is free

So I can move
Free and easy
i-n-de-pen-dent-ly.

WHO ARE YOU

Who are you
Who are you

And why are you knocking at my door

Hello
I say my name is FEAR

You can turn around and leave
from my front door

As I will not invite you in here

Who are you
Who are you

And why are you pressing on my bell

Hello
I say my name is HATE

I have come to tell you of your fate

I say

Turn around and move from my door
I have no room for HATE

Who are you
Who are you

And why are you standing out there

Hello
My name is HOPE

I think I've got good news for you
Come inside and wait right here

Who are you
Who are you

And why do you wait by my door

Hello
My name is LOVE
I have come to bring you passion

Come on in and stay with me

Who are you
Who are you

Come in LOVE and stay with me

Who are you
Who are you

Come in LOVE
Don't go away

Who are you
Who are you

Bring your passion
And stay with me

Who are you
Who are you

Come in LOVE
Don't go away

Who are you
Who are you

LOVING U IS EASY

Loving U is easy
because I love U
Using all of me
I love U with my eyes
My thoughts
My body

I love U with
My nose
My tongue
My finger tips
I love U
Using all of me

There is no part of U
I have not loved
I can not love
I love U with my entirety
I love U using all of me

I love U with my ears
My tears
I love U in my sighs
When U laugh
And when U cry

I love U love
In many ways
No matter now
What others say
I love U love
For loving me

ALONE AND ISOLATED

You walked into my life
Touched and in fec ted me
With your love
Cared for and worshipped me
Got me sweet and more than inte rested
You taught me how to smile
Helped me grow from touch ing me
You taught me how
To speak and touch you soft and ten der ly
This achieved
Like a puff of smoke
You thinned and faded away
Walked right out again
Leaving me d e f l a t e d
Alone and des p e r a t e
Alone and iso la ted
Alone liv ing
E x i s t i n g in my head
You walked into my live
When I was low in ebb

KWI

Kwi
Some time ago
You gave to me
Your left hand
I placed upon it
A gift of love
I sealed it with a kiss
I kissed your finger
Then you kissed mine
Untraditionally, unconventionally
You placed your gift of love
Upon my wedded hand
At first there were three in one
We split, so too
Was the love you gave to me
Our love got caught
Breaking two, leaving only one
Like me alone
That ring of love
Stayed on my wedded hand

FOR YOU

My blood floweth through your veins
And yours floweth through mine
I've seen you running through the rain
Forming a rainbow as you go
Your shape remaineth in my mind
The touch of your skin
The feel of your hair
With your tender touch
tells me how you care
My blood floweth through your veins
And yours floweth through mine

All of me touched your very soul
And all of yours touched mine
I still feel your finger tips
Running up my spine
You touched my soul
Made me whole and thine
You and me are intertwined
To our hearts greatest desire
My blood floweth through your veins
And yours floweth through mine

Thoughts of you occupy my waking hours
Hoping that we will always be happy lovers
Hot blood rushes through my body
Sending shivers all over me
As my thought envisioned you
your frame and mine being intertwined
Since we gave ourselves to each other
My blood floweth through your veins
And yours floweth through mine

We invaded each others tiny space
Having realised that life is but a long rat race
We hugged and sang sweet amazing grace
Hoping that we could become a one
Wishing to be in total unison
Beside each other we had lain
Thinking thoughts
Of my blood rushing through your veins
And thoughts of yours rushing through mine

EMPTY SPACE

The day you left my light went out
My world was darkened instantly
My life became dull and flat
When you walked out my world collapsed

Day light lingered not at all
My life became one cold dark night
A night that has never seen the light
Never again will my world be bright

Your absence from my life
can only bring me gloom
My world knows only doom
Since the day you left my light went out

All I wanted to do
was to scream and shout
A blanket of cloud surrounded my being
What good is it to live alone
When love is gone

Who wants to live in a world without love
The moment you walked out
I shrieked a loud shrill
People around me wondered
What my shriek was all about

But you love of my life
You were my reason
You were my light
Now you are gone the sun shines for me no more

My reason for being
Is a mere remembrance
Now love is gone I have no reason to be
Now love is gone I don't want to be me
For my life alone is filled with misery

Come back my and I'll love you for aye

Come back now and bring me sunshine in May
Come back love and put some light in my life
I want you back love for you belong to me
Your absence has brought me nought but misery

I want you back love for only then can I be
The day you walked out of my life
I knew only pain and later strife
The day you walked out of my life
A part of me died and all of me cried

That night you said good-bye
My soul mate went too
That soul mate walked right out with you
You did not walk out alone
For you took a part of me with you

That night you said good-bye
If you remained you would have heard my deepest sigh
You went on a high and left me
In dark dispair

You left dark clouds above my head
Feeling at an all time low
I want you back love
I need the comfort only you can give

I want you back love
So I can begin to live
I want you back love
Let me show you what I have to give

I want you back love
So I can truly give you me
I want you back love
So I can show you how sweet love can be
Come back my love
For love is knowing we can be

GIVE ME A LITTLE PIECE OF YOU
[FOR POPS]

A little bit of love please
That's what I ask of you
Give me a little care dear
That's what I'd like to hear
Give me a little smile please
And make it last a while

While you are there
Can I have a little um please
Can I have a cuddle dear
And a drink and cheer
Give me a little stroke please
Just to show me that you care

Can I have a little kiss dear
Before you disappear
Can I have a little time
Before you dash out of here
Give me a piece of you please
And you'll get a piece of me

Show me a little tenderness please
And appeal to my other side
Give me a little affection dear
And I might shed a tear
Show me that you care dear
And I will disguise my fear

Give me a little more love
And I will give for sure
Give me some of you please
And keep back some for you

sometimes life is sweet
some things in life are bitter
some, bitter-twisted

BUTTERFLY

In bright golden light
On a hot and sunny day
You came to
smiled
Looked around my private space
Then settled on the wall
From where
You looked at me
From the throne above my head
On which you perched
Your beautiful
Delicate
Colourful, velvet-like body
Of blue and yellow
And Green and red
You smiled at me
And in a fit
Of frenzied flight
You hovered over and
Around me
Sensitively touching me

With wings of gold
You touched my cheek
And made me smile
You loved my lips
Then stayed a while

You lovely moth
Or
Should I have said
A Butterfly

YOU ALL

Clear out of here
you are choking me
you are choking me
you're so blind
you just cant see

You are the weeds in our garden
that suffocate our loved and cherished plants
you have sucked us dry
and drained us of our energies.

you come in your many disguises
and like the prettiest of garden weeds
blend in among the flower bed
you blend in among our clan.
Then you drained us dry and transmute yourselves
you are the poison that we don't need
you are the scavengers,
that robs us of our feed.

Your kind is without shame
we all know that
we recognise the mask
that disguises your evil intentions
and watch you, every move you make.

You think us blind and unaware
we also know your smiles are insincere
Get out of here you are choking me
and you are so blind
you just cant see.

You climbed and ride our backs
to places high
this you know, dare you deny
Harsh words get spoken and then you cry.
Dry your tears, we know they're fake
and that they are shed is no mistake
you are the parasite that sucks us dry

stunt our growth and then you lie.
you're the ones ... with the attitude
show how you hate us
then you eat our food
CHECK THAT OUT
CHECK IT YET
SEE IT DEY.

REALIZATION

The condom burst
I swear

the condom burst
and the virus smiles

the condom burst
the virus smiled
my friend

the virus smiled
and I cried my friend
and I cried
my friend
I cried

The condom burst
and nine months later
a baby cried

The future waits
my friend
a future not yet seen

the future looms
whilst I sit
and cry

the future looms
and I plan
my lies.

The condom burst
the virus smiled
the future looms
a baby cried
and then
the baby smiled

my friend
the future looms
and I plan my lies.

The future looms

and all I do
is sit
and cry.

HUMAN SPONGE

I am not a bottomless pit
Nor is my main purpose here
To respond to your beckon call
I, Like you, Need to be taken care of from time to time
Handled sensitively, Given love
And respect, Whenever I'm in need of it

It is wrong of you to see me
As one who has no boundaries
Who have limitless energy
Who will respond to and meet your every need
One who will always be at the end of the line

Think a little of what is left
When you have taken all the water from the well
There will be nothing but an empty hole
Buried deep down underground
Tell me do, how do you plan to refill the well

You need to take a stock of self
And how you seem to use and abuse
Those who are kind to you
It is time you think of me
And how it feels to be used by you
And all the other yous
Who over the years have taken me for granted

Treat yourself to a sense of decency
A little self respect
And a thought or two for others other than yourself
It is wrong of you to think
I'm so naive I can not see I'm being used

Tell me do, What will be left of me
How will I find water in this deserted land
When you have drained me of my energy
Like you have the once filled well

THE BIRTHDAY POEM

According to everybody I should be happy
So everyone wishes me a HAPPY BIRTHDAY
But why should I be happier now
than I was yesterday
Or any other day for that matter
The heat of the sun is no stronger
This day than it was the last
Am I just feeling gloomy
Or is this a phase that is soon to pass
It is rather dull and gloomy out of doors
And inside I feel as if I have been
out in the wars
I sit on my own and scream out in pain
Yet you think I should be happy
The sun has not shone to warm me
Hence the reason I cannot wear
My old familiar smile
You have not phoned to greet me
The flowers in the garden are all forlorn
My bank account is empty
My love has upped and left me
And I'm feeling rather achy
Yet you think I should be happy

LET ME BE

Let me live
Let me love
Let me let my feelings out
Let me dance
Let me sing
Let me let my inside out
Let me breathe
Let me sleep
Let me lie and rest in peace
Let me look
Let me see
What this place is all about
Let me lie alone
In my lovely bed
Don't disturb my peace
When my doors are closed
Why don't you away or
Try some other day
When I might be good and well
And send you on your way to hell.

THANKS

Thank you solitude for coming upon me
When I wanted to hear my heart beat
Wanted to hear me breathe

Thank you sunshine for shining down on me
Resting on my back warming me over
Trying to turn me not brown but ebony black

Thank you sea breeze for passing over me cool,
Your tenticled fingers resting on my spine
Telling in your soft voice I should fight for you're wholly mine

Thank you all for your combined force
For working in unity pouring upon me your healing hands
Providing for me tonic for the heart and soul

Substance to make me whole food for my body and my mind
Suitable for a member of the human kind

Thanks to all of you for thinking of me a broken man
Thanks for including me in your treatment plan.

BLEATS OF SHEEP

No room for thugs in here
No room
There's no room for thugs in here
No, no room
Your space is taken thugs
No room for you in here
No room.

You can not force your way in here
You can not force your way
The door is barred to you young thugs
The door is barred to you

Don't force your way in here young thugs
You can not force your way
For if you should do young thugs
You'll surely regret you have young thugs
You'll surely regret you have

For the force beyond you young thugs
Is greater than you guessed
Is greater than you guessed young thugs

So if you forced your way in here
young thugs
You'll find awaiting you
A force from out of hell
A force from out of hell

With a whip and lash
And thump and punch
And a force of laughter

Whilst you hung your head
Like a well shamed dog
And you hung your head
To the sound bleats of the sheep
that you are meant to be
With the bleats of sheep
that you are meant to be.

DIZZY ON THIN AIR

Here I stand in a field of green
Surrounded by trees both great and small
I turn full circle and is minisculed by trees
So great, so masterful
Mountain range a mass of greenery
So too the valley below my standing point

To my right facing north an Ackee tree
To my left a Mango one
In front of me Caribbean sea
Roams in all its glory
Behind me a dip leads to the valley below

Thin fresh air I breathe me deeply
And fill my lungs to overflow
I exhale and take myself another breath
Which sends me D I Z Z Y
Here I move me F R E E L Y in the shining sun
Which warms my body through the bones
Deep into my very soul
Feeds me tonic
And colours me EBONY BLACK

Red earth
Support the fields of green
With an occasional drink of rain that falls
The fertile land supports me too
My weight expanding though it seems to be
It gives me food which comforts me
And feeds me 'til I'm full
This of course increase my energy.

DANCING IN THE BREEZE

Cool breeze from the sea

    Spin palm trees into a dance

        Twirling them in the air

    Whilst it hugs me lovingly

Hot sun aims its rays on me

    Under clear blue sky

        Tanning me on the outer side

    Whilst on the fine white sand I lie

THE HAUNTING

In the still of living room
Through the wall that joins us
Above the loudness of the music
I heard a scream so chilling
In the privacy of my own small space
First I twisted then I turned
Tormented by the thought
Of what I heard

Slowly gently I banged the wall
No response at first
I banged it louder still
You bitch slut I heard him shout
That was before the silence
That followed close behind
Patiently I await the sound of screaming
The kind that chills my soul
But still I heard the silence
Not even a sniffle could be heard
I ached deep deep inside of me
Then of course I wondered
Should I have called the police
If I did
Would they have come
Would they have come at all

TELL ME WHY

Can anybody tell me
Why people over the world are dying
From Starvation and neglect
Why mothers are dying
Leaving orphaned children behind
Who are difficult to care for
By people struggling for survival themselves

Can somebody tell me please
Is there really any need
For the growing number of people
Who are dying
From mere lack of food
When we know the world have more than we need
To feed its population many times over
If only we were less greedy
And teach ourselves to share

Can somebody out there please tell me
When we will start to teach our children
Not to think only of the self, me, mine and what I want
And teach them instead to pay a thought
For the many millions of people
Who are dying from starvation out there
Many of them living not too far from here
And if starvation and hunger is not enough
We place them under great humiliation too

Can somebody out there please tell me
How we justify our daily waste
Here in the western world
When people all around us are dying
When our daily waste could more than feed the starving
And keep more people in the world alive
Hold them back from dying
And stop ourselves from crying

Can you possibly tell me
When we can stop the hunger and starving
People digging shallow grave pits
For burying the bodies of their loved ones
Some so young, so innocent and absolutely beautiful
Why do we stand back
Watching the suffering
And the misery
On the faces of the starving ones

Can someone out there please tell me
Why it is that those who are starving
Manage to wear a smile, despite the obvious pains
And despair they must be feeling
Can any of us remember days when we complained of being hungry
But do we know what being hungry really means

Can somebody please tell me why
We have continued down the road
With our selfishness
And self possessiveness
So many people dying
So many children crying
So many people wasting
Food we can give the children
Why we have continued with our greed
When we together provide more than is enough
To meet everybody's need

I wonder if someone can tell me
How much longer we must sit and watch
People around us dropping dead like flies
Comforting ourselves with our lies
Finding someone else to blame
Without a hint of shame
Hey you, how can you justify
All your comfort eating which makes you fat
Knowing tomorrow you'll be on another failing diet
When you see starving children peering out at you
Right there through your television set

Have you not seen their tiny little legs
And their swollen bellies
The dehydration in what is left of their skin
Do you not think of their sad sullen eyes
And their often smiling faces
Tell me please, are you pleased
With the complacent stance you take
And when you say it
Do you really mean good riddance

Can someone, you, can you tell me please
Are you prepared to hang around and watch
What it is everyone else is doing
Are you one of those who say
I can't do anything about peoples' fate
Are you really prepared to wait
For more flashes on your telly
Informing you of yet another atrocity
In some distant land somewhere
If you are isn't it a pity

Can you tell me please what it would take
To move your heart of stone
To act upon some of life's disasters
That which brings about famines in certain lands
Perhaps you might be more ready to help
Those whose misfortunes
Are brought about by our very greed
And eagerness to possess a land
Rather than respond to our human needs

BRAWN NOT BRAIN

Let them try
If they can
See what it takes
To be a man

Show them a gun
See how they run
Watch them spar
In preparation for war

They are cowards really
The women say supremely
Watch them fight
Use all their might

Energy in abundance
Make themselves redundant
Preen themselves
For the preparation dance

See them now
Watch them dance
How they prance
Brawn not Brain
Is what it takes
To be a man

A WAY TO CHANGE

Work together
Love one another
Unite and fight
For human rights

Let's join hands
And make our commands
Make a date
For the state
That decides our fate

Join campaigns
Make your voices heard
Have your say
Make your desire known

That we want to change
The way things are
To how we feel
They really ought to be

We have the power
We need not be politicians
Or musicians
To bring forth change

Let's make connection
With universal organisations
Through which we can
Influence those with the power
Since we have the will

FOLD ME AWAY

My legs are ailing
My finger tips numb
My head is aching
And I need some rum

So please, please
Sep Sep Sep
Separate
Separate me from them
Separate them from me
Separate me from me

My body now bending
I can hardly stand up
I'm gripped with pain
That knows no relief

So please, please
Sep Sep Sepa
Separate
Separate me from them
Separate them from me
Separate me from me

My heart is aching
My mind is troubled
I have been dormant
But I am still unrested

So please, please
Sep Sep Separ
Separate
Separate me from them
Separate them from me
Separate me from me

I am being pulled
From corner to corner
My arms are aching
My body is ailing
So please, please
Sepa
Separate
Separate me from them
Separate them from me
Separate me from me.

SOUND AND VISION

I hear that sound again
Buzzing in my head
I hear that sound again
Going bong daga dong
I hear that sound again
Going asha sha sha sha

Bright light flashed in my eyes
Loud noises buzz through my thoughts
Spots flash in my sight
Shining as they pass by

I see that light again
Flashing before my eyes
Bright lights pass me by
Flashing before my eyes

I hear that sound again
Going do la li la li
do la li la li
I hear that sound again
Buzzing in my head

I hear that sound again
Buzzing in my head
I saw bright lights again
Flashing before my eyes
I heard that sound again
Buzzing in my head

I hear that sound again
I must be going crazy
I hear that sound again
I'm going out of my mind

Bright lights pass me by
Flashing before my eyes
Spots before my eyes
Seems I'm going crazy
Sounds buzzing in my head
Seems I'm going mad
Lights before my eyes
Shadows pass me by
Spots before my eyes
Seems I'm going mad

DIFFERENT WORLDS

The world that I live in
Is a private world
A world for me and no other
The world that I live in
Is a small world
That I share with no other
The world that I live in
Is a real world
It has no fuss
There is no bother
The world that I live in
Is a part time world
Words can not describe
The world that I live in

Your world and my world
Are different worlds you know
The world that you live in
Is a different world they say
The world that you live in
Is full of mystery
The world that you live in
Has an ancient history
The world that you live in
Is a different world form mine
The world that you live in
Knows no peace of mind
Your world and my world
Are different worlds you know

Your world
Is full of sin and crime
My world knows only peace of mind
Your world breeds
Hatred and hostility
My world knows no such insanity
Your world
Has one emotion
My world
Is full of peace
Your world
Knows only war

bird songs are so sweet
they calm the very bitter
and the twisted too

SUNSHINE SMILE

At my waking
you are there to greet me
shining bright and cheerful
when I'm groggy and only half awake
you keep me warm
and melt my frown away
set me in the mood
for a full and happy day
throughout the day you warm me
make me smile inside myself
and show my teeth
to those who care to see
what power you have to bear
you make me light a flame
inside of me
to warm some others too
Who can resist the strength you show
when they want to live
at half past nine
though still half asleep
I feel your energy
You stay with me
the whole day through
connected to your rays

You make of me what need must
and teach me how to give
shine on me oh heavenly sun
and teach me how to live.

CHRISTMAS CHEERS

Laughter from the dining room
many the people at the table
plenty the food which graced
the well dressed platter
tempting too the smells
coming from the busy kitchen
cheery the noises
at the now opened champagne
frothing, fizzes in the up held glasses.

Cheers, Cheers
and merry Christmas to everyone

was all that one could decipher
from the myriad of noises in the busy dining room.

On the table sat many serving dishes
empty plates waiting to be filled
piled up high with the wonderful spread
placed upon the well set table

From where I stand
I can see the carved up turkey,
beside it sits more dishes
containing beef, pork and chicken
then in a corner all forlorn
sat a dish with a lone nut roast
all this food waiting to be eaten.

Then comes the banging sounds
from Christmas crackers now being pulled.

Screaming and shouting from excited children
laughter by the adults gathered
as they downed yet another drink.

No thoughts for the murders
of that which graced the table
which has formed their Christmas feast.

SEARCHING FOR SELF

Oh loves
How sad your lives become
You once so strong and shining
Now a glimmer of the light you were
You who used to touch the souls of many
Being kept controlled under cover

What of the fight you used to have
What so your independent spirit
How so you allowed yourselves to be oppressed
Once I knew you found yourselves
That was before you were thus discovered

Now you hang your heads in shame
Waiting, hoping, that someone will discover you
You've lost yourselves after having found you once
Keep on seeking, try to find yourselves again
If you can't do that

Then, place yourselves so you may be found
By someone else if that is what it takes

RAIN IN TUNISIA

First there was the darkened sky
followed by a clap of thunder
and then a flash of
lightening lit the sky
like an array
of fireworks fantasia.

One enormous drop of rain
followed by another
caused a tickle in the nostrils
as the huge drops
hit the hot dry earth.

Squawking loudly
a grey male pussy cat
came flying in for shelter
as if thrown
by some amazing force
meowed so loudly
as he complained
about being caught out in the rain

People sat and stared
making comparisons
of rain-fall in their homelands
to that in Tunisia
All looked in amazement
at the changes in the weather
so warm, so beautiful
and together so amazing.

PROSPERITY

Prosperity is mine
if only I can reach and claim it
Prosperity is mine
and you don't have the right or power to withhold it
Prosperity is mine
and that I shall have
For I am prosperity
and prosperity is me.

WORDS

Words are FOODS
Smell them
Taste them
Chew them
Swallow them
Digest them

Words are KNOWLEDGE
Read them
Learn them
Remember them
Know them
And use them

Words are MUSIC
Feel them
Listen to them
Play your beats to them
And let yourself
Dance to them

Words are WEAPONS
Arm yourself with them
Try to form them
Reshape them
Defend yourself with them
And win your battles of life with them

FUN TIMES ALONE

Alone is never awful
Alone is always good
Alone is not being lonely
Alone is taking time for self
Alone is preparation
For time we spend with other
Preparing for the crowding
Invasion and what we don't control
Alone is like being with others
When you're having fun
Not under dark rain clouds
But in the shining sun
Alone is taking time out
From a cluttered day
Alone is feeling comfy
In your very own company.

ATLANTA MORN

At dawn I awoke to a chorus
of singing birds flitting from tree to tree
rays of golden sunshine peeping through
the creek where the curtains meet
whooshing sound of breeze
as it lashes on the wall nearest to my head
each morning in Stone Mountain
I smiled as I stirred at the crack of dawn
seeing the start of yet another day
feeling pleased to be alive
in a land where golden sunshine pours
out its strength on one like me.

THE JOURNEY

From deep in the thicket of the bush
on some distant shore
some of our ancestors were plucked
and taken to waiting ships
They were dragged and chained
and beaten to a pulp
barked at when kind words would have done
a chase of hate started
that old familiar journey
for the me that I am

For from one of those aged ancestors
the me have descended
born some thousands of miles away
from the land where those ancestors dwelt

Through the cruelty of those ages
I speak me now a different tongue
from my forebears [on the original shore]
my customs to them are alien

Of my culture, they think I have me none
so it is
for my language was forcefully denied
and for to speak it
those folks were severely punished
for attempting to hold on to some distant past
Oppressors tried [in vain] to break their spirits
but it could not be done
it was too hard for them to break a practiced one
instead they took our names
and gave us of their own
Hence some of us are known as Mary Jones
and others Jimmy Brown
being forced to leave behind us
those sweet sounding A FREE CAN names.

SHE SPOKE MY NAME

Emerging from a darkness
That far superseded that of a dungeon
A darkness much darker than a moonless night
A darkness in which it was hard to
Distinguish night from day

I entered a world of mist and fog
In which I was surrounded by heavy
Dark oppressive rain clouds
Struggling to reach the light
I sweep away at these clouds
The more I see the more oppressed I felt

I gave up struggling
Gave in to my oppressed state
I sat waited patiently
Looking gaunt
Feeling wrecked
I was tired and worn

Time passed me by
Suddenly, I felt a glimmer of hope
I blinked
And lo, there was light before my eyes
One more blink
Then I saw a single rose
More blinks then a bunch of flowers
Appeared before my eyes

In my silence and despair
I heard a rustling sound
The wind whispered my name
It said SEMBA
SEMBA I am calling you

Surprised and astonished
I looked around
And there I saw
The familiar face of my friend
Who whispered
It is me
SEMBA It is me
I smiled

Suddenly I became aware
That the sun was shining
This, because its rays
Penetrated my world of darkness
Bringing with it a warmth
A warmth I had long forgotten

Sunshine once again returned into my life
Once again life had a purpose
Yes I found a reason
A reason to go on living
A person a friend to share my burden
The load I carry on my back

your life was so sweet
tinged with what was bitter
as for what's twisted?

LIFE IS A MOVING THING

Life is a moving thing
And you have to move in time
Keep to the beats of the rhythm
Of the opening dance
Life is a moving thing
Which does not stand still
So you have to keep in time
To the rhythm and the beat
Life is a dance
So you better learn to prance
And twist and move around
Life is the thing that
Keeps us on the move
Life is a day on the move
When the sun goes down
Life is the smile that I wear
When my ebb is low
Life is the love that you give
On a cloudy day
Life is the love that you make
When you're wide awake
Life is what happens
When you reach ecstasy
Life is what happens
Between you and me.

POEM FOR ALAN
[GIN AND TEARS]

For whom do I shed the tears
I cry
Is it for you my past love
Who broke to me
News of a common friend
Is it for him
Whose life has been so abruptly ended
No time to say good-bye
No time to bid farewell
No time to try explain
To love ones and friends
That which so worried him
Is it a result of the gin I drink
The gin and bad new that sting my eyes
Is it because of that I cry

ODE FOR ALAN

Alan why did you do it
Why did you do it man
Could you not have talked
To Chris or Susan
Could you not have talked
To Keith or to John
Alan why did you do it man

Could not have waited
For another break of day
Another dawn when you would
Have heard the songs of birds
From where you were
Could you not have
Tried to ring the Samaritan
Could you not have found and held
On to the strength we know you had
Alan why did you do it man

Why did you end that which you had
[That is life] in the midst of living
Why have you left a hole
In the lives of those you touched so lovingly
In the time you spent with them
Did you not know that the sun would shine again
For you tomorrow
Alan why did you do it man

Damn and blast
You have robbed yourself of a life
You should now be living
You've robbed your friends of jokes
That you should with them be sharing
Damn and blast
Alan why did you do it man

It's been a long time
Since we shared a laugh
It's been a long time since
We had a talk
And now those things cannot be had
You could have talked to
Chris and Susan
You could have talked
To Keith or to John
Alan
Why did you do it man.

THOUGHTS FOR ROSE

Words are cheap
not expensive
unless we give them freely
exclusively
words are power
and live on forever and ever
they feed and nourish us
and give us energy
they can empower us
if we let them thus
so Rose hold on to these
and increase your e n e r g y.

DON'T DO IT

Don't take their childhood
away from them

Don't force them to grow
before their time

Don't force their legs
and rob them of their innocence

Don't get drunk
then brutalise the children

Don't take their innocence
then place your guilt on them

Don't you dare
You son of a bitch

Do all of these
then tell your children

That you r e a l l y, t r u l y
T r u l y, r e a l y do love them

And he spake to me of love

He said

Remember your children
are not your children

Try to protect
and not abuse them

Your special gift your children